ה

MW01039651

The Divine
Commandments

The Significance and Function of
the Mitzvot in Chabad Philosophy

by
Nissan Mindel

Published by
KEHOT PUBLICATION SOCIETY
770 Eastern Parkway / Brooklyn, New York 11213

THE DIVINE COMMANDEMNTS
(formerly published as The Commandments)

CONTENTS

INTRODUCTION

Judaism governs every phase of the Jew's life and work, from the cradle to the grave. The Jewish religion is not something distinct from, or added onto the Jewish people; it is their very essence as a people. It is their way of life, as well as their life, because Jewish existence without the Torah is simply inconceivable.

The Jewish religion was given to the Jewish people almost simultaneously with their freedom as an independent nation. The Divine Revelation on Mount Sinai took place only seven weeks after the Exodus from Egypt.[1]

The Divine Revelation on Mount Sinai took place in the presence of *all* Israel. Witnessing the occasion were six hundred thousand men, aged between twenty and sixty, plus women, children, old people and the multitude of alien slaves and nobles who accompanied the Jewish people at the time of the Exodus. In all, there were several million eyewitnesses to the Giving of the Torah on Mount Sinai. Thus, the Jew's firm belief in the Torah and the Divine Commandments it contains is not a matter simply of faith, but of absolute conviction. To quote Maimonides (*Hilchot Yesodei Hatorah*, ch. 8):

---

1. The Exodus took place on Nissan 15, 2448 (in the year 1312 before the Common Era). The Revelation on Mount Sinai took place on Sivan 6, seven weeks later.

"Not because of the signs that Moses performed did Israel believe in Moses…but at the Revelation on Mount Sinai, when our own eyes, and not a stranger's, saw; when our own ears, and not anyone else's, heard the fire, thunder and lightning; and he (Moses) entered into the cloud, and the Voice spoke unto him, and we heard, 'Face to face did G-d speak unto you….' Thus, they to whom Moses was sent were the witnesses to his prophecy…."

Maimonides goes on to say that should any "prophet" attempt to refute the prophecy of Moses by any sort of "proof," we would not listen to him, for it would be the same as if someone were to try to convince us about something despite what we had seen or heard with our own eyes and ears. We should regard his "proof" as nothing but trickery and deceit.

The author of *Sefer Hachinuch*[2] says in his preface: "It is the established practice of all civilized peoples of the world to accept the evidence of two or more witnesses as conclusive proof, even to the extent of sentencing a man to his death…. That is why G-d gave the Torah to Israel in the presence of six hundred thousand male adults, so that they could bear testimony to the fact."

As for the generations following the Revelation on Mount Sinai down to our present day, all those generations of Jews who did not themselves see the Revelation but heard about it from their fathers and grandfathers, acceptance of the Torah is for them not just a matter of trust and tradition. It is a fact, the authenticity of which has been continually reaffirmed by the daily prayers and the observances of the commandments by the Jewish people, generation after generation.[3]

---

2. Lit., "Book of Education," this is an anonymous work on the 613 *mitzvot*, following their order in the Torah, believed to be authored by R. Aharon of Barcelona. First published in Venice, 1523.
3. *Derech Emunah*, p. 64a (Poltava, 1912; new edition, Kehot, 2003) by R. Menachem Mendel of Lubavitch (1789-1866). Grandson of R. Schneur

The author of *Sefer Hachinuch* argues that it would be foolish and unreasonable for anyone to reject this historic evidence and to decide to reason it all out by himself. Human research has not even fathomed the secrets of the physical forces concealed in nature, let alone metaphysical science, which is largely beyond the grasp of the human intellect.

Our fundamental beliefs[4] concerning the Torah and Divine precepts are these: That G-d, who gave the Torah to Israel through Moses, is the First Cause, without beginning or end; that He created all existing things out of nothing (*creatio ex nihilo*), and that nothing is impossible for Him to do; that He has no helpers of any kind; that He knows everything that man does and rewards him according to his deeds; that by observing G-d's commandments, man will merit everlasting happiness; that the Torah was given together with its explanation, which is the one we now have by tradition from generation to generation—the explanation contained in both the Babylonian and Jerusalem Talmuds, and in several other works of early Jewish sages, such as *Sifri*, *Sifra*, *Tosefta* and *Mechilta*, etc.[5]

The Torah contains 613 Divine commandments, embracing every possible phase of Jewish life. These commandments are divided into 248 positive precepts—*do's*, and 365 negative precepts—*do not's*. The former, our Sages say (*Tanchuma Hakaddum (Bober)*, *Tetze; Talmud, Makkot* 24a; *Zohar* I:170b), equal the number of organs in the human body; the latter—the number of blood vessels (also the number of days in the solar year). The number of the positive and negative commandments is significant, because when we observe the

Zalman of Liadi, he is known as the "Tzemach Tzedek" because of his famous responsa under that name.

4. For a more exhaustive study of the subject see Maimonides, *Commentary on the Mishnah, Sanhedrin* 10:1; also *Emunot Vedeot* by R. Saadiah Gaon, *Sefer HaIkkarim* by R. Yosef Albo, etc.

5. *Sefer Hachinuch*, Introduction.

248 positive commandments, each bodily organ fulfills its Divine duty; similarly, when we do not transgress any of the 365 prohibitions — as we might be tempted to do by the desire that flows through our body — each one of our blood vessels remains free from pollution. Thus, by observing *all* the Divine precepts, we cause the entire human entity to rise above the level of the animal, and to attain the highest plane of human perfection.

The 613 Divine commandments are only the principal laws of the Jew's code. Each one of these laws has by-laws and regulations contained in the *Oral Law* (Talmud, etc.), which we now have in classified and concise form in the *Shulchan Aruch*.[6] These laws are final; they cannot be changed or modified, and any "reform" of the Jewish religion is contrary to the spirit of the Torah and Judaism.

In their immediate objective, the commandments are generally classified into two principal groups: a) Laws governing human relations, and b) Laws governing the duties of man toward the Creator.[7]

The ethical value of the laws governing human interaction as stipulated by the Torah is admired even by those who are not inclined to believe in revealed religion. Nevertheless, many laws governing the Jew's daily behavior are difficult to understand even for those who are ready to accept the Torah as the word of G-d. To a person who has not studied Torah, some laws might seem irrational, and out of step with the present world. However, anyone who has learned about the significance and purpose of the commandments will

---

6. Lit., "Prepared Table," compiled by R. Yosef Caro (1488-1575), supplemented by the *Mappah* ("Tablecloth") of R. Moshe Isserles (1520-1572; known as *Remo*).

7. This classification is a very ancient one, e.g. in the last *Mishnah* of *Yoma*: "For transgressions that are between man and G-d the Day of Atonement effects atonement, but for transgressions that are between man and his fellow the Day of Atonement effects atonement only if he has appeased his fellow."

know better. To say that you believe in a G-d who can reveal His will, and at the same time to choose the commandments according to your own judgment is, according to Maimonides, to claim to be "more perfect than the Creator."[8]

In other words, ethics and morality that are not based on the idea of G-d and the Torah are, to say the least, abstract ideas, having no criteria by which to be measured. Ethics becomes a relative and changeable conception: what may be regarded as "ethical" by one person may be regarded as "unethical" by another, and what may have been regarded as "moral" in the last generation may be regarded as "immoral" in the present. It is undoubtedly true that the separation of ethics from religion is at the root of the evil which has caused one world conflagration after another.

On the other hand, "piety" means cleaving to G-d and "imitating the ways of G-d," which, in turn, mean to seek and practice lovingkindness, justice, and righteousness. But there can be no true "piety" unless the laws governing human relations, as prescribed by the Torah, are strictly followed.

Classifying the commandments in his own way into fourteen groups,[9] Maimonides makes it clear that *all* Divine precepts, without exception, have a specific purpose, aiming at the perfection of the body and soul, since a pure spirit can dwell only in a pure body.[10]

However, the welfare of the body can be secured only by following the precepts prescribed by the Torah, in which the laws aiming at this end are treated most carefully and most minutely. These laws, including the laws of kashrut, Sabbath observance, charity, and all the social and ethical precepts, form the bulk and core of the Torah, and make for true moral perfection.

---

8. *Guide to the Perplexed* 3:31.
9. Ibid., 35.
10. Ibid., 31.

In his concluding remarks to the *Guide*, Maimonides says, "...the perfection in which man can truly glory is attained by him when he has acquired—as far as this is possible for man—the knowledge of G-d, the knowledge of His Providence, and the manner in which it influences His creatures in their production and continued existence. Having acquired this knowledge, he will then be determined always to seek lovingkindness, judgment and righteousness, and thus imitate the ways of G-d."

Here we see again how, according to Maimonides, laws governing human relations and those governing the duties of man toward the Creator are inextricably bound.

From the above we can also see that the fulfillment of G-d's commandments is essential to gain a clear intellect and a higher perception of G-d, a concept which is repeatedly emphasized in the Chabad philosophy. For the precepts are the will of G-d, and since "G-d's will and essence form a single oneness,"[11] one attains the highest union with G-d through obeying His commandments. Moreover, as we shall see later (in chapters two and seven), this connection to G-d through the observance of the precepts is attained regardless of whether or not the worshipper "understands" their deeper significance.

In the course of the following treatise, an analysis will be made of the general significance and purpose of the Divine commandments which the writer has gleaned from the principal sources of Chabad philosophy. No attempt will be made to point out the significance of any individual commandment, nor does the writer claim to present in the course of this brief discourse an exhaustive analysis of all the esoteric significances and functions of the Divine precepts, concerning which it is written: "My thoughts are not like your thoughts" (Isaiah 55:8) and "Can you by searching under-

---

11. Maimonides, *Hilchot Yesodei Hatorah* 2:10.

stand G-d?" (Job 11:7).[12] It is hoped, however, that even this brief outline will go a long way toward enabling the layman to understand the deeper significance of the Divine precepts in general.

12. *Tanya*, ch. 2. The *Tanya* (name derived from the initial word of the book) is the principal philosophical work of R. Schneur Zalman of Liadi, in which the principles of *Chabad Chasidism* are expounded. Also called *Likkutei Amarim* ("Collection of Sayings") or *Sefer shel Benonim* ("Book of the Intermediate"). First published in 1797 and reprinted over five thousand times, it has also been translated into many languages. A bilingual English translation was first published by Kehot in 1973.

The author, R. Schneur Zalman ben Baruch, Talmudist, codifier and philosopher, founder of Chabad-Lubavitch Chasidism, author of the (Rav's) *Shulchan Aruch,* was born in Liozna, Russia in 1745, and passed away near Kursk, Russia in 1812. His other works include *Torah Or* (Torah Light), *Likkutei Torah* (Torah Gleanings; see also below, ch. 5, note 9), *Biurei Hazohar* ("Commentaries on the *Zohar*"), and *Siddur* with Chasidic discourses.

CHAPTER ONE

Self-Restraint and Divine Discipline

Discipline, whether in the army, school, or home, aims to create the best possible conditions under which the highest results can be attained. The soldier, student, or child may not appreciate the necessity of all the minute rules and regulations forming the code to which he is subjected (and at first glance, they might seem nothing but restrictions on his personal freedom). It is nevertheless equally useful for him to submit himself to this code, whether or not he knows the full implications of each one of the rules and regulations it contains.

When the child grows up, or when the soldier finds himself on the battlefield under enemy fire, he will realize the importance of his training, and no measures will be necessary to enforce the code of laws which he may have been unwilling to follow previously. Until he is able to judge the merits of the discipline which has been enacted for his benefit, however, he must accept it without question.

The commandments, in their most elementary function, are likewise a code of discipline laid down by G-d for the human race. Indeed, the first condition of the commandments is man's absolute submission to the law of G-d—*kabbalat ol malchut shamayim*, submitting to the rule of the kingdom of Heaven. In Chabad philosophy, this submission is carried a degree further to *bittul hayesh*, surrender of the ego, which is achieved by mature reflection on the greatness of G-d, His sublime exaltedness, and overpowering majesty; for in the presence of the Almighty G-d, a person must feel a sense of crushing insignificance and humility. At the same time, however, one's heart is filled with a passionate adoration for the Divine majesty, and a yearning to cleave to Him. Thus, a person becomes aware of a series of emotions with regard to G-d, such as awe, respect, love, adoration, and surrender. These emotions, all of which stem from the intellect, find expression and satisfaction in the observance of the Divine *mitzvot*: the sense of awe will make him abstain from transgressing the Divine prohibitions, and the sense of love will make him fulfill all the positive commandments of the Torah with devotion.[1]

Were we human beings purely spiritual beings, we would find ourselves constantly in a state of *kelot hanefesh* — yearning of the soul to cleave to the Almighty, which would make the existence of our Divine soul in an earthly body impossible. But we were not made that way. We are a synthesis of the earthly and the heavenly, consisting of an earthly body and a Heavenly soul. Our earthly body is subject to all the earthly desires and pleasures common to all animals, but we people are also subject to temptations to which no animals are subject.

---

1. The process of these spiritual reactions is outlined in the *Tanya* as follows: The soul consists of two component parts: the intellect (*sechel*) and the attributes (*middot*). The intellect comprises three faculties: *Chochmah* (wisdom), *binah* (understanding) and *daat* (knowledge), hence CHaBaD. *Chochmah* is the first flash of wisdom. When this wisdom is elaborated by analysis, erudition and mature reflection, it is said to have given birth to *binah*. From *chochmah* and *binah*, *daat* is born; this is the stage where one has arrived at fixed ideas and conclusions.

   The three faculties of the intellect (CHaBaD) are the source of the attributes, the latter being "born" of the intellect, for it is after mature reflection on the greatness of the Divine Majesty that fear and love of the Almighty, and all other spiritual attributes, will take place. (*Tanya*, ch. 3; *Iggeret Hakodesh* 15, where the subject is treated at greater length.)

Whereas an animal will seek merely to satisfy its natural needs, dictated by its instincts for existence and procreation, man will often be tempted to indulge to excess in the satisfaction of these same needs. Such overindulgence is harmful to the body as well as to the soul, and the Divine commandments are the best safeguard against such self-destruction.

Now, of course, G-d could have created man a "perfect" creature, free from any temptation, and unable to do evil at all. He could have made men and women who were full of brotherly affection and utterly unable to harbor any ill feeling, envy, or hatred. Obviously, however, this was not the Divine purpose. G-d did not want to have this world inhabited by a race of robots. It was G-d's wish to give a person the free will to do both good and evil, and it is G-d's desire that a person should subjugate his evil inclinations and do good. It is not remarkable for an angel to do nothing but good, but it is remarkable when a human being, consisting of a physical body imbued with earthly desires and temptations, conquers his evil inclination and subjugates it to the worship of G-d.

However, without G-d's help, it would be all but impossible to attain the victory of the soul over the body. That is why G-d gave us the Torah and the commandments; that is also why He has endowed us with a Divine soul and high intellect.

However, herein also lies a grave peril. Since our Divine souls give us dominion over all other creatures and even the forces of nature, we can easily abuse our great powers and apply them in a direction contrary to the will of G-d; for has not G-d given us a free will to do as he pleases?

We are all the more liable to go astray because we are not always aware that there is a Supreme Master. Or, we may tell ourselves that if there is one, He has abandoned His masterpiece, the world, to His choicest creature—man—as, indeed, some people would have us believe.

Because of the Divine design or purpose of Creation (to which we shall refer at greater length in a later chapter), it is inevitable that, under the influence of our quest for material pleasures, the Divine power and ever-watchful Eye is usually screened from our perception (otherwise, it would be very easy to be good). As a result we can be misled to think that there is no Higher Authority to whom we will eventually have to account for our deeds. Man's powers to harness the forces of nature for his use often give him a sense of self-importance, bordering on sheer arrogance. Such erroneous notions give us free license to do as we please, so long as we have the power to do so. Indeed, technical development and scientific attainments have so far outstripped moral and ethical advancement that the result has been the breeding of modern tyrants and dictators, surpassing in cruelty and savagery anything the ancient "uncivilized" and unscientific world ever produced.

The Divine commandments are, therefore, intended in the first place to act as a restraint upon us, so that we will not overreach ourselves. They remind us that we are not the *owners* of the world but merely its *trustees*. We have been entrusted by the "lord of the manor" to manage the estate. We must both develop it, and protect it from any damage or destruction.

Clearly, anyone submitting to the Divine commandments, accepting them as such, and fulfilling them with a simple sincerity, faith and humility, cannot possibly fall into debasement of character. By the very act of fulfilling a Divine commandment, we become aware of the existence of G-d, and are reminded of the presence of G-d. The more frequently we perform the Divine *mitzvot*, the more frequently we will be reminded of G-d, until the awareness of G-d will become constant with us, a sort of second nature.

Indeed, there are a number of commandments which are specifically stated to serve as "reminders," "signs," or "memorials." The commandment of wearing *tzitzit* (fringes), for instance, is a reminder of all the commandments of G-d (Numbers 15:39). The *tzitzit* are like an insignia given by a king to signify the wearer's allegiance to him,[2] or like a uniform reminding the wearer of his rank and special duties. A *mezuzah* serves as an emblem or "coat of arms" of a Jewish home. Shabbat, with its prohibitions on all kinds of labor and many other restrictions, is a "sign" or "memorial" of the Creation, and of the miraculous liberation from Egypt.[3] Of course, serving as a sign or reminder is not the only purpose of these commandments, for they share with all others many profound meanings and functions, known and unknown to us. (Some of these deeper meanings of the precepts will be pointed out in subsequent chapters.) However, these commandments do emphasize clearly the fundamental function of the precepts as the code of Divine discipline.

We have already mentioned that the commandments, in a general sense, tend to educate people in self-restraint. Temperance and moderation are some of the finest qualities of the Jew. Chabad Chasidism places much emphasis on this point; it teaches moderation in natural appetites, passions and even language. Clearly, such laws as *kashrut* are designed to train us in abstinence, besides being also the best health laws. But Chabad goes even further than that, urging moderation even in things permissible. "What is prohibited one *must* not do; what is allowed, one *should* not do,"[4] for overindulgence in things permissible is also harmful, even if

2. *Sefer Hachinuch* (see above, *Introduction*, note 2).
3. See *Shabbos,* published by Merkos L'Inyonei Chinuch, New York; *Tefillin* by Alexander Cowen, published by Merkos L'Inyonei Chinuch. See also *Tzitzit* by J. Immanuel Schochet, by the same publisher.
4. *Hatamim,* Issue 5, p. 101 (Warsaw, 1937; Kfar Chabad, 1971; 1984), quoted in the name of R. Schneur Zalman of Liadi. Also in *Hayom Yom,* 25 Adar II (anthology of aphorisms and customs arranged according to the days of the year; assembled by the Lubavitcher Rebbe, Rabbi Menachem M. Schneerson, from the talks and writings of his father-in-law, Rabbi Yosef Y. Schneersohn. New York, 1943, Heb./Yid. Bi-lingual English Edition, Kehot, 1988).

not quite so harmful as indulgence in things not permissible.

Self-restraint is very hard to accomplish, and requires one's constant vigilance.

> "It is indeed a great, fierce struggle to break one's evil nature which burns like a flaming fire…therefore, every man according to his station and standing in the worship of G-d should weigh and search himself whether his service of G-d measures up to this hard battle…. In regard to positive worship (prayer, blessings, grace, study of the Torah, charity, etc.) one should make a determined and relentless effort to overcome the obstacles placed by the 'animal soul' within him, preventing him from the fullest concentration and devoutness…, and he who forces himself to study the Torah a little more than his natural inclination (or to give charity a little more than usual), has already won a small battle…. Similarly, in regard to abstaining from evil, one should check himself in the act of participating in idle gossip, and refrain from making an uncomplimentary remark about someone else even to clear oneself…and especially (one must be on one's guard) in cases where there is no actual prohibition, but concerning which our Sages said, 'and they shall be holy,' (Leviticus 21:6)—sanctify yourself (by abstention) in things permissible (*Talmud, Yevamot* 20a)."[5]

It is often more difficult to exercise self-restraint with regard to things permissible than in regard to things prohibited, since in the case of the former there is no legal restriction. But even things permissible join forces with evil unless they are dedicated to the service of G-d. For example, when one eats kosher food not for the purpose of being strong to serve G-d but for his own indulgence and pleasure, the energy derived from this food *temporarily* lends strength to the forces of evil until such time when the person

---

5. *Tanya,* ch. 30 (free rendition).

decides to apply this energy to something good and constructive. It is not so when one eats non-kosher food, the energy of which joins forces with evil *permanently*, and will be released only "in the end of days," when G-d will destroy death forever (Isaiah 25:8) and the unclean spirit will be passed out of the land (Zechariah 13:2)—unless the transgressor attains full and absolute repentance in his own lifetime. The very terms *mutar*—permitted, and *assur*—prohibited, are derived from verbs denoting "released" and "chained" respectively, the former being free to be applied to both good and evil, and the latter permanently "chained" or "imprisoned" by the evil forces.[6]

We can see with what profound earnestness the Chabad philosophy approaches the question of self-discipline in every phase of the Jew's life. And while the ideal of "sanctifying oneself by moderation in permitted things" may seem to the average man rather remote, there are the Divine precepts of definite prohibitions and commands (*do's* and *do not's*) which, when observed, place man well on the road to the highest degree of holiness.

SUMMARY: Man's imperfection, caused by his split between a physical and spiritual self, is part of the Divine plan. We have been given the ability to ignore the will of our Supreme Master, indulge our earthly desires, and abuse the great powers which G-d has given us. Such a path would be harmful, both to our body and our soul, subjugating the latter to the former. However, G-d has given us a set of Divine commandments, which, if followed earnestly and diligently, will ensure the welfare of our bodies, train us morally and spiritually, build our character, and remind us both of our proper place as mere trustees of our world and of the existence of G-d, the true Master of the Universe. Fulfillment of the Divine precepts is the first step in man's advancement toward spiritual perfection.

6. Ibid., ch. 7.

CHAPTER TWO

Connecting with G-d

The principal function of the commandments, however, is more than that of keeping people within proper or appropriate bounds and under control. The *mitzvot* are not intended to make a person a mere drudge. Although absolute obedience and surrender are fundamental aspects of the commandments and primary conditions of any true worship of G-d, the commandments are at the same time intended to elevate the worshipper to a higher plane through the very act of worship. For the commandments are the means of establishing contact between man and G-d. Even among humans, any personal contact and relationship between two persons of unequal status creates a real sense of elevation in the person of the lower rank. How infinitely more can men and women benefit from a "relationship" with G-d.

Mitzvah—commandment—also means companionship or union[1] (compare the Aramaic *tzavta*—companionship). One who fulfills a commandment becomes united with the essence of G-d, Who ordained that precept. This is the meaning of the Mishnah (*Ethics of Our Fathers* 4:2) "the reward of a mitzvah is the mitzvah," for

---

1. The English to enjoin—to enjoin obedience—has the same meaning.

the greatest reward of the worshipper is the very communion with G-d, which is attained through the fulfillment of the precept. This concept can be better
understood by the example of a simple, uneducated
man, without any wisdom or intellect whatsoever, so
much so that he does not even realize how far removed
he is from any kind of wisdom (for even such realization
is a certain degree of wisdom). Now, as far as an intellectual of the highest rank, whose whole essence is cen-
tered on the abstract, is concerned, this ignorant man
simply does not exist.... Let us assume now that such a
great scholar requests this ignorant man to do something
for him. Immediately, this man acquires an existence
both in his own eyes (seeing that he was requested by
the great scholar to do something, and that he is able to
carry out the scholar's request), and also in the eyes of
the scholar.... It is of no importance what that particular
request is, for the important factor is the very request
and its fulfillment.... Thus, a commandment a) gives a
higher existence to the drudge and b) places the Com-
mander and the commanded in a mutual relationship.[2]

Moreover, the effect of the fulfillment of the Torah and
its precepts goes beyond the limits of a mere relationship; it
leads to an absolute communion with G-d.

The *mitzvot* are the will of G-d, which He willed us to
fulfill. The Torah is the wisdom of G-d. Since "the Essence of
G-d, and His will and wisdom form a single oneness"—because there can be no plurality in G-d—it follows, therefore,
that by our study of the Torah and the exercise of His commandments, we are in absolute communion with G-d.

To be sure, the Divine will and wisdom are "clothed" in
material things, that is to say, through the use of material

---

2. R. Yosef Y. Schneersohn of Lubavitch in a letter, published in *Hatamim*,
Issue 1, p. 25, and subsequently in his *Igrot Kodesh*, vol. 10, p. 368. Also
in *Hayom Yom*, 8 Cheshvan (see above, ch. 1, note 4).

objects, for example, in *tzitzit*—wool, in *tefillin*—leather, etc.—objects which seem to be greatly removed from the Divine Being. However, the union with G-d is not affected by their substance. It is like embracing the king, when it does not matter how many garments the ruler is wearing, since the body of the king is in them. Similarly, when one is embraced by the king, it matters not that the king's arm is clothed.[3]

The far-reaching effects of this relationship and connection with G-d will be discussed later. For the moment, we shall consider *how* this connection takes place through the fulfillment of the *mitzvot* and the study of the Torah.

The relationship between Israel and G-d through the medium of our religion is explained in the *Zohar* as follows:

"Three are interlocked together: [the People] Israel, the Torah and the Holy One, blessed be He, and all are on different planes, one higher than the other, partly hidden, partly exposed."[4]

The meaning of this saying is that the three—Israel, the Torah and G-d—are linked together like a chain of three rings, of which the upper part of the bottom ring is held by the lower part of the middle ring, and the upper part of the middle ring is held by the lower part of the top ring.

In each of the three rings there is a hidden part and a visible part. Similarly, there are apparent qualities and latent qualities in each of the three: Israel, the Torah and G-d....

The manner of their union is twofold:

a) The revealed qualities of Israel unite with the revealed attributes of G-d by means of the revealed part of

3. *Tanya*, ch. 4.
4. Comp. *Zohar* III:73a.

the Torah, and the latent qualities of Israel unite with the latent attributes of G-d by means of the latent part of the Torah;

b) The revealed qualities of Israel are connected with the hidden qualities of Israel, and the hidden qualities of Israel in turn unite with the revealed part of the Torah; the revealed part of the Torah is connected with its esoteric part, and this in turn unites with the revealed attributes of G-d; finally, the revealed attributes of G-d are connected with His hidden attributes and thus the union is completed.

It follows therefore that this union with G-d is present in every Jewish person, man or woman, young or old, whether learned in the Torah or ignorant of it. At the same time, however, there are various factors which influence the *feeling* of this union, either strengthening it or weakening it.[5]

In Chasidism the commandments are termed "the *garments* of the soul," and the Torah is termed "the *food* of the soul." Just as physical food and clothing are necessary for the welfare of the body, so are spiritual food and clothing necessary for the welfare of the soul.

The soul has three forms of expression: thought, speech and deed. When a person observes the commandments of G-d *in deed*, discusses the deeper meaning and significance of the commandments through *speech*, and concentrates, and grasps all that his intellect is able to grasp of the deeper meaning of the Torah through his faculty of *thought*, his soul becomes *fully clothed* in the Divine commandments,[6] and is, therefore, in perfect unity with G-d.

---

5. *Some Aspects of Chabad Chassidism* (revised edition—*On the Study of Chasidus—A Trilogy of Chasidic Essays*, 1997, pp. 7, 11, 12 (translation of a letter by Rabbi Yosef Y. Schneersohn, sixth Lubavitcher Rebbe, dated 25 Nissan 5696, and published in his *Igrot Kodesh*, vol. 3, p. 533 ff.)).
6. *Tanya*, ch. 4.

The study of the Torah, although it is an "outer garment" like any other commandment, is likewise the "food" of the soul. For when the intellect "digests" a certain point of law in the Torah, it takes in, so to speak, the Divine wisdom, which becomes the soul's very "flesh and blood," like food digested by the body. Hence the expression of the Psalmist (40:9), "Your Torah is within my inner parts."[7]

This connection with G-d through the Torah and commandments means for the Jew's soul what vitamins, calories, adequate shelter, and clothing mean for his body, and more. For while these physical elements are required to sustain the body, connection with G-d is the very essence of the Jew's soul.

SUMMARY: The purpose of G-d's *mitzvot* is not to turn us into robotic figures, but to elevate us so that we can develop a relationship with our Creator. We can, in fact, create an unbreakable link between ourselves, the Torah, and G-d. A union exists between every Jew and his Creator; our task is to strengthen this connection by means of the Torah and the commandments. Using physical terms, we can consider the latter as what we wear and the former as what we eat. Just as we need real-life food and life to exist, so we need their equivalents for our spiritual well-being.

7. Ibid., ch. 5.

CHAPTER THREE

The Purpose of Creation

The question "What is the purpose of the Creation?" has engaged the attention of thinkers and philosophers of all ages. This question is closely linked with the question "What is man's function in the design of Creation?" As may be expected, Chabad deals with both of these questions at great length.

Briefly, the explanation is as follows:

Before the universe was created, there was only G-d alone, the perfect Unity, filling all "space," including the "space" of the world subsequently created.[1] G-d remained unchanged after the Creation. What was new were the created things which received existence and life from His Infinite Light[2]—only after the Light and Life emanating from

---

1. The term "space" used here is not to be understood literally, since the very existence of "space" is a creation; however, this is not the place for an elaboration of the subject (see *The Four Worlds*, Kehot 2003).
2. Divine Revelation is termed in Chabad *Or Ein Sof*, the Light of the Infinite (or the Infinite Light), since the very essence of G-d is inconceivable. "Just as the soul fills and animates the whole body, so does G-d fill and gives life to the whole world. But can we say that the *entire* essence and function of the soul is to sustain the body? Similarly, we cannot say that the entire essence of G-d is that He creates and sustains the worlds and

Him had been so "reduced and minimized" as to be in a po-
sition to give life and energy to earthly and corporeal creations. Thus, a series of worlds were created, one "coarser"
than the other, successively concealing the Light and Life
emanating from the Creator, until there came into being our
own material and corporeal world, which is the lowest
(where the Divine Light is most concealed), and the darkest
of the dark, so much so that it is possible for things to exist
in this world which are in defiance of G-d.[3]

Since our world is the last and "lowest" in the chain of
Creation, below which there is no other, it follows that our
material world is the main object of Creation.

Moreover, the chain of the various worlds, one lower
than the other, cannot have been created for the sake of the
higher worlds. For, as created entities, the Light of G-d radi-
ating within them is less than at its Source.[4] They can never
rise above the level at which their status has been permanently fixed. Rather, the chain must have been created for
this, our lowest world, where man was given the power to
subjugate the forces of evil, and to turn darkness into light—
a light which would seem brighter by virtue of the very con-
trast with darkness. In this way man was given the
opportunity to rise above the level of even the higher worlds.[5]

Similarly, it is logical to deduce that the human being is
the object of our world, since we were the last to be created,
being preceded by the animal kingdom, the vegetable kingdom and the mineral kingdom.

Furthermore, since our world is the goal of Divine Rev-

---

all its creatures. Here lies a great deal that is inconceivable to the human
mind" (*Some Aspects of Chabad Chassidism* (*On the Study of Chasidus*, p.
10)).

3. *Tanya*, ch. 36.
4. The Hebrew word for "world" is *olam* (עולם), bearing similar letters to
heelam (העלם), the Hebrew for "concealment."
5. See ibid.

elation, and man is the object or goal of this world, it follows that the fate of the world is closely linked with that of man.

Our Sages said (*Tanchuma, Nasso* 16), "G-d desired to have an abode in the lower world" ("lower"—in the sense of corporeality, as we have explained above). Rabbi Schneur Zalman[6] explains this statement in the following words: "It was His will to derive pleasure from the subjugation of the *sitra achara*[7] and the conversion of darkness into light."[8]

"It is in the nature of the good to do good."[9] G-d is good, and therefore, G-d gave existence and life to the worlds and creatures. Now, of course, G-d could have stopped short of our world in the process of Divine emanation, and could have concluded the Creation with the higher form of creatures such as the angels. But a candle shines brightest in the dark and "the superiority of light is most appreciated in comparison with darkness."[10] It was G-d's desire that He be recognized even by earthly and material creatures, and that the "light" of G-d be revealed in this dark world by the subjugation of the forces of "defiance."[11]

Herein lies the function of a human being. When a person eats and drinks, not for the simple purpose of satisfying hunger and thirst, like an animal, but with the intention of having strength to fulfill the Divine laws; when he toils and labors not merely to live in comfort, but to comply with the commandment of charity—in order to enable others to live as well—then the food he eats and digests, and the energy he

6. See above, *Introduction*, note 12.
7. *Sitra achara*—lit., "the other side"; this is a Kabbalistic term for all forces of evil not being "the side of holiness" (*Tanya*, ch. 6).
8. *Tanya*, ch. 36.
9. *Emek Hamelech, Shaar Shaashuei Hamelech*, beg. ch. 1; *Shaar Hayichud Veha'emunah*, ch. 4; *Shomer Emunim*, 2:14, by R. Yosef Irgas (1685-1730), quoting the Kabbalists. See also *Chacham Tzvi* (Responsa), 18, by R. Tzvi Hirsch ben Yaakov Ashkenazi (1660-1718).
10. Cf. Ecclesiastes 2:13. See *Tanya*, ch. 26.
11. Ibid., ch. 36.

derives therefrom, are applied precisely to the purpose of converting the material into the spiritual.

Moreover, when a person fulfills his duty and mission in life, not only does he attain his own goal in the scheme of Creation, but he also helps the rest of the world around him, including the animal, organic, and inorganic "kingdoms," to attain theirs. For everything that has been created in this world was placed at our "service." We depend on the other forms of life (including the inanimate, which also possess a "Divine spark" that gives it energy and keep it in existence[12]) for our sustenance. When, for example, we apply the energy we derive from a glass of milk, to the fulfillment of our mission in life, then the cow from which the milk came, the meadow upon which the cow has grazed, the very glass from which we drink the milk, and everything and everybody associated with the production of the milk and its conveyance from the farm to the refrigerator, have fulfilled their mission. Conversely, if one uses his energy to cheat, kill, or to otherwise violate the word of G-d, he has not merely failed to fulfill his duty in the design of Creation, but he has also caused damage to himself as well as to others and to the world around him.[13]

SUMMARY: Our world was the last in a series of creations in which the Divine Light and Life were diminished. It is the furthest away from its Divine source, and hence the lowest in the series, one in which the Divine Light is especially concealed and where evil can dwell unimpeded. Our world exists for one purpose: to allow man to overcome these forces of darkness and to create a "dwelling place" for G-d in our lower world. We accomplish our task by doing good, by consciously fulfilling G-d's laws. Thereby, we simultaneously attain a degree of perfection and help the other "kingdoms" reach their goals.

---

12. *Shaar Hayichud Veha'emunah*, ch. 1.
13. *Tanya*, ch. 37.

CHAPTER FOUR

The Source of Life

G-d gives existence and life to the universe and everything that exists. He is the Source of all Life.

All existing things have a Divine "spark" that gives them life and keep thems in existence. Were G-d to deprive them of this Divine "spark," they would dissappear. This "spark" is termed *koach hapoel banifal*, "the force of the Creator active in the created." It is like a stone flying upwards in the air, which continues on its course as long as the power of the throwing hand is still active in it; when this power ceases, the stone falls back to Earth. Similarly, as G-d created things out of nothing (*creatio ex nihilo*), they can exist only as long as the Divine power creating them is maintained in them. This is the meaning of the words we say in our daily morning prayers, "He, who in His goodness each day, constantly renews the work of the Creation." In other words, there is a constant flow of "life" from the Source of all Life—from G-d—to this earth.[1]

The wellbeing of the world depends upon the fulfillment of the Divine purpose in the Creation—namely, that it serves as "an abode" for Him—and this condition can be brought

---

1. *Shaar Hayichud Veha'emunah*, ch. 2.

about only by the fulfillment of the Divine *mitzvot*. In other words, by doing so, we cause a greater flow of life to descend upon this world from the Source of Life. For all things exist by the will of G-d; the precepts are the will of G-d; the will of G-d is the cause of this world; hence the precepts are the Source of Life.

Therefore, when we fulfill the Divine *mitzvot*, we bring down Divine benevolence upon ourselves and the world around us. Herein lies the special significance of each particular mitzvah, which is determined by the particular "reaction" that the mitzvah evokes. For all precepts have their counterpart "on High," so to speak. For example, when we stretch forth our hand to give the poor man a donation, G-d "stretches His hand forth" to bestow kindness upon us and upon the world; when we look compassionately upon the less fortunate, G-d "looks compassionately" upon us and the world around us. Of course, we must not understand this literally, for there is no corporeality in the Divine Being, but the "reaction" is there nevertheless. Moreover, this "reaction" in bringing down Divine benevolence through the fulfillment of the Divine precepts is brought about whether or not we know what it is in reference to each precept.

It is the same when we abstain from committing any of the prohibitions, when the resulting "reaction" is to evoke corresponding Divine powers to rid the world of all evil.

Thus, the fulfillment of the Divine *mitzvot* has a dual effect: on the one hand it elevates all physical matter to its highest form, and at the same time it draws down life and Divine benevolence upon this world. We may not know how and in what form this Divine "reaction" is brought about, but we may be sure that the observance of every mitzvah and the abstention from every prohibition surely produce a Divine "reaction" which brings us life, benevolence and true happiness in this world, as well as in the World to Come.

Although this may sound like quite an abstract idea to those who are far removed from the study of the Torah and the observance of the daily *mitzvot*, it is a matter of fact to those who do study the Torah and do observe the *mitzvot*; for these people *feel* an inner bliss and spiritual satisfaction which cannot be explained in words, but must be *felt* to be appreciated.

This Divine light in its revealed or perceivable form, as one draws it upon one's self through the fulfillment of the Divine precepts, is generally referred to as the *Shechinah* (Divine Presence).

Shechinah is derived from the words *veshachanti betocham* "I shall dwell among them" (Exodus 25:8), for it is the original radiation of the Divine Light which is revealed in the worlds, and from this source comes the individual degree of Light and Life to all things (created) in accordance with their due.... The Life and Light emanating from this source is merely in the form of *radiation*, like the light coming from the sun (which is not the sun itself). However, the *Shechinah* itself—the very origin of the revealed light and its source—which is the source of all existence and life, is something that the (finite) worlds are incapable of enduring. Were they to receive the light of the *Shechinah* without its being screened and concealed in a "garment," these worlds would cease to exist, being "absorbed" by their source (as the sun's rays at their source are lost in the sun itself, since no sun rays can be seen there but the body of the sun). What is this "garment" which can conceal the *Shechinah* and "clothe" it so that the light may be endured without expiration? It is G-d's will, wisdom, etc., which are "clothed" in the Torah and its *mitzvot* that are revealed to us...and together with it (the Torah and precepts) comes the *Shechinah*...."[2]

Thus, when one studies the Torah, his soul and only its two inner "garments" (faculties of expression)—

---

2. *Tanya*, ch. 52.

speech and thought—are absorbed within the Divine light and united with the Divine Being in perfect unity, causing the *Shechinah* to rest upon his Divine soul. Our Sages said (*Berachot* 6a), "Even where a single person is engaged in the study of the Torah the *Shechinah* is with him." But in order to bring the light and radiation of the *Shechinah* to rest also upon his body and "animal soul"...it is necessary to fulfill the practical *mitzvot*, performed by the body itself. In this way the actual power of the body engaged in this act is absorbed into the Divine light and will, uniting with Him in perfect unity. This is the (function of the) third "garment" of the Divine soul—*deed*.... This increased Divine Revelation, brought about through the performance of a mitzvah or the study of the Torah, does not, of course, imply plurality or change in the Divine Being, as it is explained in the Talmud (*Sanhedrin* 39a): A certain heretic asked Rabban Gamliel, "You say that the *Shechinah* rests on every assembly of ten. How many *Shechinahs* have you?" To which Rabban Gamliel replied with an analogy of the sun's rays entering many windows, etc.[3]

SUMMARY: When we fulfill the Divine *mitzvot*, we are acting in accordance with the Divine plan, and we are helping to create a dwelling place for our Creator down here on earth. Each mitzvah we perform—and every misdeed we do not perform—elevates us and brings a distinct kind of G-d's benevolence down upon us, creating an equal reaction on High. This Divine Light, as we perceive it in its semi-hidden form, is the *Shechinah*, the source of all existence and life. Without the *Shechinah*, brought down by the study of Torah and the performance of practical, life for us would be inconceivable.

---

3. Ibid., ch. 35.

CHAPTER FIVE

Physical and Spiritual

We have already stated[1] that all things created in this world have a purpose of their own in the scheme of Creation, and that by fulfilling the Divine commandments, man does not merely attain a state of perfection, but at the same time elevates the rest of the world around him—his *share* in this world—from a low state of corporeality to the higher state of spirituality. In other words, man, by using his energy in compliance with the Divine will, automatically brings about a state of affairs in which all other energy-producing creatures and objects—in the organic and inorganic "kingdoms"—contribute to the realization of the Divine purpose of the Creation; that purpose, very simply expressed, is the victory of good over evil.[2]

We will now consider this subject a little more deeply, in order to get a better appreciation of the importance of physical things (religious articles like *tefillin, tzitzit, lulav,* etc.) in the fulfillment of the Divine precepts.

In the order of things created on this earth we find the following sequence in Genesis: the earth, or the mineral

1. Ch. 3.
2. Ibid.

kingdom; the flora—all kinds of plants; the fauna—all kinds of birds and animals; and lastly—man. Thus, we have a general classification of life on our earth into the "four kingdoms": inorganic, plant, animal, and man.

These "four kingdoms" mark their scale of development in the order in which they were enumerated: plant life being on a higher scale than inorganic matter, the animal kingdom being higher than plant life, and man—highest of all.[3]

This relative development of the "four kingdoms" is due to the relative manifestation of the Divine power or "spark" which animates all things created. We can discern this Divine "spark" least of all in inorganic matter which *apparently* has no "life" at all, and most of all in man who has an immortal soul, which is a "part of the Divine above."[4]

However, this is true only from the point of view of the *relative manifestation* of the Divine factor in them, that is to say, as far as the human intellect can discern it. In reality, however, viewed from "Above," all things alike came into being by the word of G-d, and the same power of *creatio ex nihilo* keeps them in existence.

Contemplating the greatness of the blessed *Ein Sof*,[5] the thinking person will understand that as this name (*Ein Sof*) indicates—there is no end or limit to the light and vitality that spread out from His simple Will, and which is united with His essence and being in perfect unity.

Had the worlds descended from the light of the blessed *Ein Sof* without "contractions," but gradually descending step by step, by means of cause and effect, this world would not have been created in its present form, in a finite and limited order....

3. *Tanya*, ch. 38.
4. Ibid., ch. 2.
5. See above, ch. 3, note 2.

The contractions are a way of obscuring and concealing the flow of light and the life force, causing the light and vitality to come down to the lower creatures in small amounts, so that creation could be in a finite and limited state....

So, indeed, is the quality of this minute illumination, which provides the higher and lower worlds with sustenance and life.

Now compare it with the quality of the infinite light, which is concealed and does not exercise its influence in the worlds in a revealed manner to provide them with life, but encompasses all these worlds from above.

Of course, it does not mean that this light actually encircles and encompasses from above *spatially*, but rather as far as the revelation of this influence is concerned...

To illustrate this point, consider this material world. Even though, "The whole world is full of His glory," which refers to the infinite light of the blessed *Ein Sof*, nevertheless only very limited life force—of no more than that of the inanimate and vegetable worlds—is clothed within the world in the form of "revealed" influence. The majority of the light of the blessed *Ein Sof*, however, is described as "encompassing" the world—although it does actually pervade it—since its influence is not revealed further in the world, but affects it in a hidden and concealed manner. And any influence of a concealed nature is referred to as "encircling from above."[6]

In other words, there are two forms of Divine emanations termed in Kabbalah as *"memalei"* (filling) and *"sovev"* or *"makif"* (encompassing), which Chabad philosophy explains as follows: The former, *memalei*, is the Divine Revelation which is so "contracted" as to be able to be "clothed" or confined within (hence "filling") material and finite objects.

6. From *Tanya*, ch. 48 (free rendition).

This is the Divine emanation in its revealed form, which Revelation is expressed in *giving energy to* the created things in their finite state. The second emanation, the *sovev*, is the Infinite Light, which is so strong that it could not be confined to finite objects, and is therefore said to "encompass" them.

In other words: All created things consist of substance and form, which are indivisible. If, however, we were able to imagine the substance of a thing as separated from its form, we would say that the *substance* comes into existence by the Divine emanation we call *sovev* or *makif*, whereas the form comes into existence by the Divine emanation we call *memalei*.

To return now to the "four kingdoms" mentioned above, we can see that this gradation is conceivable only for the Divine factor termed *memalei*, for the greater the degree of the *revealed* vitality of the thing, the higher its place in the scale of Creation.

The varying degrees of Divine light and life that gives life to the created things do not, of course, imply plurality or change in the Divine Being, as we have already mentioned before.[7] We can see this also from our own body. Our soul or living spirit fills our entire body, from head to foot. Our soul is certainly one indivisible unit. Yet, its *vitality* differs in different parts and limbs of the body: it is strongest in the intellect, the seat of which is the head and which is manifest in thought, and less in other organs, such as the foot. Yet, when the idea of taking a walk is conceived, the foot moves instantaneously—a fact which shows that the will is in *potentia* in the entire body, in the form of an "encompassing force."[8]

---

7. Ch. 4.
8. *Derech Mitzvotecha, Tzitzit,* 15a (a Chasidic exposition of the precepts by R. Menachem Mendel of Lubavitch, author of "Tzemach Tzedek." Poltava, 1911; new edition, Kehot, 1991; see above, *Introduction*, note 3).

Thus, in all things created, from the highest spheres to our own most corporeal world, there is a combination of the *two* kinds of Divine emanation, the *creative* (*makif* or *sovev*) and the *energizing* (*memalei*). The former is the infinite and concealed Divine factor, and the latter is the finite or "revealed" factor (in the vitality of the thing). These two Divine factors are contained in all things in a certain ratio. The greater the preponderance of the energizing factor in any particular object, the higher its grade in the scale of development *as we see it*. By the same token, the more primitive or corporeal a thing is, the stronger is the *creative* force in it, and the less of the energizing factor. It follows, therefore, that from the point of view of the Infinite Light, the more primitive objects stand above the less primitive or (from our point of view) the more "advanced," for the former contain more of the "Infinite" power which is necessary to keep them in existence. For example, suppose we are viewing a flowerpot, with a bee perched on one of its flowers. In *our estimation* the earthen pot is the lowest in the scale of creation, the flowers are in a higher class, the bee in a still higher, and we in the highest class of all. But let us imagine we could see the Infinite or *creative* force in them; then we would classify them in reverse order.

Viewed from this point of view, it will become clear why man is dependent for his existence upon the other forms of life on this earth, and particularly upon the earth itself. For at first glance it seems paradoxical that bread should be able to sustain man, for bread is seemingly so infinitely inferior to man who has a soul in him. But now that we have seen that in the origin of creation, inorganic matter possesses a greater force of the *sovev*, it is not surprising that all things depend upon the earth for existence. Accordingly, this is the meaning of the words of the Torah (Deut. 8:3): "Not by bread alone does man live, but by everything that proceeds out of the mouth of G-d does man live"; that is to say, it is not the physical bread that sustains man, but the Divine word, or power, which enables bread to exist in a state of *creatio ex ni-*

hilo, that sustains man. It is this same Divine word that keeps the human organism in existence. As we have said before, the Divine *factor* is strongest in the inanimate, and consequently bread has the Divine power to sustain man.[9]

We can now see the importance of the various religious articles, no matter how humble their physical origin, in the Jew's worship of G-d. For by using them, the Jew brings about the highest possible Divine Revelation in this world. At the same time, he attains the highest possible contact or communion with the Divine Being, because the other forms of creation contain a "higher spark" in their origin than his own human organism.

Every Jew has his own "share" in this world, in which it is his duty to bring forth Divine revelation. For just as he is dependent upon his share in this world for his *physical* existence, that same "share" is dependent upon him *spiritually,* for it is only through his agency that it can serve the Creator's purpose.

In the light of the above, the meaning of the well-known saying by the founder of Chabad, "G-d transforms the spiritual into something material, and the Nation of Israel transforms the material into something spiritual,"[10] will be clear.

---

9. *Likkutei Torah, Mattot* 81b. The *Likkutei Torah* is a series of Chasidic discourses by Rabbi Schneur Zalman on the weekly portions, *Shir Hashirim* and festivals, beginning with *Vayikra,* but preceded by discourses on *Beshalach* and *Pekudei.* It was published in the year 1848 in Zhitomir by R. Menachem Mendel, author of "Tzemach Tzedek," and is attributed to him because of his commentaries, notes, and explanations of the discourses of his grandfather. Actually it is the second volume of *Torah Or* by R. Schneur Zalman (see above, *Introduction,* note 12) printed first in the year 1837 at Kopust, when only the first volume (on the first two books of the Pentateuch, also Chanukah and Purim) was printed, because the printing house at Kopust, together with many other Jewish printing houses, was closed by order of the government. The second volume was subsequently printed under the name of *Likkutei Torah* (*Hayom Yom,* 3 Shevat).

10. *Hayom Yom,* 27 Elul (see above, ch. 1, note 4).

SUMMARY: All things that exist contain two kinds of Divine emanations. The first is the creative force, which is infinite and hidden. The second is what gives anything in existence its energy; this emanation is finite and visible to us. Everything that exists contains these two emanations in different proportions. From our limited vantage point, we would see something with a greater proportion of "energy" as being higher on a scale of development. As far as we are concerned, therefore, there is an upward progression to the four "kingdoms" from mineral to vegetable to animal and finally to human. However, from the point of view of The Infinite, the situation is reversed. The smaller the percentage of "energy" anything has, the larger percentage of infinite creative force it must have. This strange paradox explains why we are dependent on animal and plant life for our sustenance, and why mundane objects like tefillin—made from parchment and leather—can help us in our worship of G-d.

CHAPTER SIX

The Reward

Belief in Divine retribution, that is, reward for good deeds and punishment for wrongdoing, is one of the fundamental doctrines of our religion. It is the eleventh article of our faith as formulated by Maimonides.

It is obvious that were Divine retribution to follow instantaneously man would be deprived of his greatest gifts—free will and independence of action. He would fear to do anything wrong on peril of immediate punishment, and he would be eager to do good out of selfish motives, being tempted by the immediate compensation that would follow a good deed. This was not G-d's idea of man's life upon this earth.

In order that man retain his full measure of independence of action, it was necessary that Divine retribution be concealed, even to a degree in which doubts may be raised as to its very existence. Indeed, the question of "Why do the wicked prosper?" (Job 12:1) has been often voiced, and many a man has been misled to believe that there is no Divine Providence at all, but that everything occurs by chance. But study and reflection will show that only man's short-sightedness and mental limitations can give rise to any doubts about Divine retribution. Even where the human mind is at its best and highest, there is still an immeasurable distance between our finite mind and the infinite wisdom of the Creator. To the logical person, it is unthinkable that "the Judge of all the earth should do no justice" (Genesis 18:25), and the absolute faith of Abraham, the first Jew, in G-d's justice, irrespective of any inconsistencies that one's mind might conjure up, was inherited by us, his children, forever.

What form does reward take?

Our Sages have distinguished between *two* kinds of reward: the "revenue" (*perot*—fruits) and the "capital" *(keren):* "These are things whose fruits man enjoys in this world, while the capital is laid up for him in the World to Come: honoring father and mother, deeds of lovingkindness, making peace between man and his fellow, etc." (first *Mishnah* of *Peah*[1]). Maimonides in his commentary on this *Mishnah* states clearly that every favor man does to his fellow brings him reward in this world.

Such compensation is derived not only from the improved society—since one good deed is emulated by another—but there is also special individual compensation for each act of kindness shown to one's fellow man that is also acceptable to G-d. (Misguided kindness is clearly excluded.)

> It is known that man's arousal of his own spirituality in this world—when he calls forth in his heart the feeling of kindness and compassion toward all who are in need of these qualities—evokes a similar reaction on High. Thus abundant mercies from the source of mercy and the life of all life, blessed be He, descends downwards upon him, going from the higher to the lower worlds, until the Divine benevolence is clothed in this material world in (the blessings of) children, life, and sustenance.[2]

Therefore, every act of lovingkindness which may be in-

1. See also *Talmud, Shabbat* 127a.
2. *Iggeret Hakodesh,* 17.

cluded under the general term of *tzedaka*—charity (or in the words of our Sages—*gemilut chassadim*, acts of loving-kindness) calls forth a reciprocal act of benevolence from on High (see also ch. 4, above). So much for the "revenue" of a mitzvah, which is enjoyed in this world.

There is, in addition, the "capital" of the mitzvah, which applies to *all* commandments, and particularly to the duties of man towards his Creator, such as *tzitzit, lulav,* etc. This reward is reserved for the World to Come, for it is so great, so infinite, that it cannot be "clothed" in this corporeal and finite world. It is with regard to this reward that our Sages said: "The reward of a mitzvah is not in this world" (*Talmud, Kiddushin* 39b).[3] Even where it is written in the Torah "in order that it may be well with you" (Deut. 22:7 *et al.*), our Sages say (ibid.) that what is meant by these words is "the world that is all good," that is to say, the "World to Come" in afterlife. For all worldly pleasures, even assuming an entire lifespan full of them, without a moment's vexation or suffering of any kind, could not be sufficient reward for fulfilling a single commandment. Said our Sages (*Ethics of Our Fathers* 4:16), "One moment of pleasure in the World to Come surpasses all the pleasure of an entire life in this world." The Sages continue (ibid.) that "this world is like a vestibule of the World to Come; prepare yourself in the vestibule so that you may enter into the hall." The same idea is expressed in the saying, "He who labors before the Sabbath (meaning in this world) will eat on Sabbath (in the World to Come)" (*Talmud, Avodah Zarah* 3b).

The real reward, then, is to come in the Hereafter. But what is the nature of this reward? Is it conceivable that a simple act, such as putting on *tefillin*, wearing *tzitzit*, or giving a few cents to charity, should result in such abundant compensation that this whole world could not contain it?

---

3. *Iggeret Hakodesh*, 3.

We shall discuss the second question first. It is explained by the founder of Chabad Chasidism in the following simile:

> The earth possesses the fertility to produce all fruits according to their kind. These fruits are brought forth by planting seeds in the earth. Now, these seeds have no taste or sweetness of their own; nor does the earth contain the form of the fruit, since various fruits can be produced, depending upon the kind of seed planted. However, through the union of the seed with the earth, the earth's growth potential can be "clothed" in the seed to produce the proper fruit. The same is true of the commandments which…are like seeds without taste, having been incorporated in material things, for example, *tzitzit* made out of wool, *tefillin* on parchment, etc., for they contain the Supreme Will, and through Israel who fulfills and practices the *mitzvot*, the Supreme Will flourishes and grows to be revealed….[4]

Herein lies the explanation of the lofty potential with which each mitzvah is charged. A mitzvah is like a seed. If a tiny seed can contain the possiblity not merely the substance and form of one tree, but of innumerable trees, each one containing the seeds for further growth *ad infinitum*, is it not conceivable that a Divine precept, no matter how small or insignificant it may seem to us, should similarly contain infinite Divine "Light" and "Life"? The precept is the Divine will which is the essence of life; all that is required to bring it out from potentiality into reality is the act of performance of the mitzvah, such as the Jew's putting on *tefillin*, or wrapping himself up with a *tallit*, which corresponds to the act of sowing the seed in the earth.[5]

Thus, by performing acts like these, we sow the seed, the

4. *Torah Or, Shemot* 53d.
5. Ibid.

fruit of which we shall reap in the World to Come in the form of the *real* and *everlasting* reward.

We now come to the consideration of the nature of this reward which is stored up for us in the World to Come. There, the nature of this reward is the pleasure of *perceiving the essence of G-d*,[6] something we are not able to do in this world. At present our eyes of flesh and blood are able to see only physical matter. We are not able to see the Divine "spark" that gives existence and life to all things surrounding us. We are able to see the outer form, but not the inner essence of a thing. In the Hereafter, however, we will be given the ability to perceive G-d in His true essence, and this pleasure is something we cannot even imagine.

Of this pleasure, Maimonides says:

> As the blind man cannot perceive the shade of color, nor the deaf man the strain of sound, so the physical body cannot comprehend the spiritual pleasures (derived in the Hereafter), which are continuous, everlasting, and uninterrupted; these pleasures have nothing in common with, nor any relationship whatever to, the pleasure derived from material things. The nature of this pleasure is the conceiving of the essence of the Creator...in the Hereafter, where our souls become cognizant of the knowledge of the Creator. That pleasure is indivisible, indescribable, and there is nothing that has any semblance to it; it can only be referred to in the words of the prophet when he wished to express his admiration for this eternal joy, "How abundant is Your goodness!" (Psalms 31:20)—this is the eternal good and final purpose (of life on this earth)....[7]

Referring to the subject of reward, Nachmanides[8] is of

---

6. Comp. *Kuzari* 1:109 and on.
7. Maimonides, *Commentary* on *the Mishnah, Sanhedrin* 10:1.
8. Nachmanides, *Shaar Hagemul.*

the opinion that the time of the Resurrection of the Dead is the final *Olam Haba* (World to Come), after which there will be no more death. The "Hereafter" preceding it—although its spiritual pleasure and reward are of the nature and degree described by Maimonides (quoted above), insofar as they are capable of description—is the transitional period between death and the time of the Resurrection of the Dead. The Resurrection, as the culmination point of Creation, infinitely surpasses in spiritual pleasure and Divine Revelation even the Hereafter (or *Gan Eden*, Paradise).[9]

On this question, Chabad takes the view of Nachmanides, because it is also the view of the Kabbalah.[10] Furthermore, Chabad explains the seeming anomaly that there could be a greater understanding of G-d while the soul is clothed in a body than when it is free from it. The reason for this strange situation is that it is in the nature of *Gan Eden* for the soul to enjoy and grasp "the glory of the *Shechinah*."[11] Now, a soul is something created by G-d, and no creature, not even the angels, can altogether conceive the essence of G-d.[12] Even in the highest worlds, the Divine "light" is covered up, as otherwise even the angels could not endure it, and could, therefore, have no existence.[13] However, when the soul inhabits the body, the study of the Torah and the fulfillment of the Divine will enable man to reach the highest understanding of Divine Revelation possible in this world. At the same time, these actions provide the Jewish People with the strength to experience this Divine Revelation— without any screens whatsoever—in the World to Come,

---

9. In this, Nachmanides differs from Maimonides who believes that the era of the Resurrection (the revival of the dead) is a transitional period before the *Olam Habba*. (See Maimonides, *Hilchot Teshuvah*, chs. 8, 9; also *Hilchot Melachim*, chs. 11, 12).
10. *Derech Mitzvotecha, Tzitzit*, 14b.
11. *Iggeret Hakodesh*, 17.
12. *Tanya*, ch. 36; *Iggeret Hakodesh* 23.
13. *Tanya*, ch. 36.

after the Resurrection. For this purpose, G-d gave the Nation of Israel the Torah, which is called "strength." (Indeed, something of this Revelation had already been experienced at the Giving of the Torah on Mount Sinai.)[14]

When the days of Moshiach come, and particularly when the dead shall rise again, the world will have reached its highest perfection for which it was originally created. Then Israel will perceive, even with eyes of flesh and blood, the essence of the Creator, as it is written (Isaiah 30:20), "And your Master will no longer conceal Himself, and your eyes shall see your Master." From this abundant light to Israel, the darkness of the entire world will be illuminated, as it is written (Isaiah 40:5), "And the glory of G-d will be revealed, and all flesh will see...."[15]

We can now understand why the soul is sent down to inhabit a body, despite the fact that for the soul it is a great regression to leave the presence of the *Shechinah* on High, and come down to life in a material world, where the light of G-d is utterly concealed. No wonder the soul does so unwillingly, inasmuch as the soul itself is perfect, and needs no chastisement in this earthly life for its own sake.

However, the general purpose of the soul's descent to this earth is to "repair" the world, and transform it from a material one into a spiritual one, where the Divine light shall be revealed without any "screens," and to subjugate the earthly matter to the spiritual form, in order to "make this world an abode for G-d." Through the observance of the Torah and *mitzvot*, a Jew purifies his own earthly body, enabling him to connect with G-d, At the same time, he also purifies his "share" in this world, and prepares it for its highest perfection in the World to Come when the spirit of evil will be eradicated, "the glory of G-d will be revealed," and "all the earth will be filled with G-d's glory."[16]

14. Ibid.
15. Ibid.
16. Ibid., ch. 37.

SUMMARY: There are two kinds of rewards for the good deeds we do when we are alive, one for which we can see the reward in this world, and one for which the reward is reserved in *Olam Haba*. When we act with kindness towards others who are properly in need of our compassion, or when we try to improve the world around us, we create a better society for all of us, and we benefit from that. We also cause a reciprocal reaction from the Heavens; this response may bring us blessings in this world in the form of prosperity, health, and general well-being. There are other *mitzvot* that we do for which we receive no reward in this world, for the simple reason that the reward for them is so great, it cannot be contained here, but must be reserved for the World to Come. There we will finally be able to perceive G-d's essence, something inconceivable in the world we know.

CHAPTER SEVEN

Sincerity — the Keynote of Divine Worship

Although the idea of Divine retribution rightly provides an incentive for the fulfillment of the positive commandments and a deterrent from transgressing the prohibitions, the ideal worshiper is, of course, the one who worships G-d with no thought of reward or punishment, but simply because the Divine precepts are good and truthful *per se*.[1] Our Sages advise us (*Ethics of Our Fathers* 1:3), "Be not like servants who minister to their master upon the condition of receiving a reward, but be like servants who minister to their master without the condition of receiving a reward." There is the story of the rabbi who could buy an *etrog* only on condition that he relinquish to the vendor the rights to the reward of this mitzvah in the World to Come. The rabbi cheerfully did, exclaiming, "Now at last I will be able to perform a mitzvah without regard for the *Olam Haba*!"[2] And of Rabbi Schneur Zalman, the founder of Chabad, it is told that he exclaimed in moments of ecstasy, "I do not want Your *Gan Eden*, I do not want Your *Olam Haba*; I want only You, You alone!"[3]

1. Maimonides, *Hilchot Teshuvah*, ch. 10.
2. Comp. R. Shlomo Y. Zevin, *Sippurei Chassidim — Moadim*, p. 262 (quoted in *Torat Menachem — Hitvaaduyot*, vol. 11, pp. 21-22).
3. *Derech Mitzvotecha, Shoresh Mitzvat Hatefilla*, ch. 40.

Such is the highest kind of Divine worship—it is prompted by *love*, as differing from the worship prompted by *awe*. We have been commanded to have both love and awe of G-d in our heart, and both are the "offspring" of *chochmah, binah,* and *daat* (Chabad).[4] However, the worship prompted by love is undoubtedly of a higher rank.[5]

Nevertheless, considering the lofty functions of the Divine precepts as discussed in the previous chapters, it is clear that the important part about the precepts is their *fulfillment.* Though the knowledge of the functions and significances of the commandments is very important, making for a higher form of Divine Revelation,[6] such knowledge is not essential to the fulfillment of the precepts. What is important is *faith* in G-d, and a sincere desire to cleave to Him,[7] and these are qualities that are found in the unlearned as well as in the scholarly worshiper. Indeed, with regard to G-d, we are all unlearned and ignorant, as King David said (Psalms 73:22), "I am ignorant and unknowing."[8] Every Jew, without exception, has an innate love for G-d, which is an inheritance from our fathers, and that is why even the least observant Jew is able to sacrifice his life for the sanctification of G-d's name.[9]

The Chasidic view that the common, unlearned Jew can be as good, and sometimes even a better worshiper than the scholar was something of a revolutionary idea, which caused a great deal of ill feeling among the learned men of the period.

4. See above, ch. 1, note 1.
5. Maimonides, *Hilchot Teshuvah,* ch. 10.
6. *Tanya,* ch. 38. Elsewhere, using the simile of the seed (see above, ch. 6), the precepts performed without *kavanah* are likened to uncultivated fruits while the precepts performed with *kavanah* are likened to cultivated fruits, which are of a much superior quality.
7. Ibid., ch. 41; *Likkutei Torah, Nitzavim,* 50d.
8. *Tanya,* ch. 18.
9. Ibid.

For centuries it had been the accepted view that the saying of our Sages (*Ethics of Our Fathers* 2:5), "*Lo am haaretz chasid*" (the ignorant man cannot be a pious man), must be taken literally, and must be rather rigidly accepted. The result of this interpretation was that the ignorant man—*am haaretz*—was held in contempt and despised. This attitude was undoubtedly a strong factor in reducing ignorance and illiteracy among the Jews, but it did create two distinct types: the scholar—the *talmid chacham*, and the ignorant one—the *am haaretz*.

During the centuries of exile, and particularly during the Medieval era, when the economic plight of Jews everywhere was at its worst, the proportion of the people who were unlearned grew larger. Jews were scattered all over the world, often in isolated areas, where the means and opportunities for Jewish education were meager or lacking completely. Many were unable to send their children to *Yeshivot*, and under economic stress the standard of Talmudic education deteriorated considerably.

Now, life was very hard for these simple, unlearned folk, for not only did they suffer from the oppression of their non-Jewish neighbors, but also from the disdain of their own fellow Jews—the scholars. Yet, despite their lack of knowledge and scholarship, they clung to their faith with a devotion unsurpassed by their scholarly brethren; they worshiped G-d as best as they knew how, but with all their heart and soul.

When the Baal Shem Tov[10] first began his activities, he turned his attention first to the economic plight of his brethren in Eastern Europe, and then to their spiritual plight. He began by "healing the body first, and then the spirit."[11] It is not within the province of this treatise to dwell at any length upon the scope and success of the pioneer work of

10. R. Yisrael Baal Shem Tov, founder of Chasidism, b. 18 Elul, 5458 (1698), d. Shavuot, 5520 (1760).
11. *Hatamim*, Issue 2, p. 44.

the Baal Shem Tov, that of his successor, the Maggid of Mezritch, and the latter's disciples, among whom Rabbi Schneur Zalman, the founder of Chabad-Lubavitch, ranks foremost. This, however, should be said, that the warm attitude toward the simple, honest Jew is one of the fundamental principles of Chabad. Paradoxical though it may seem—for Chabad, meaning *wisdom, understanding, knowledge*, is a highly intellectual study—the idea that *all* Jews have a soul which is a "part of the Divine above," and consequently, even the unlearned Jew has inherent qualities on a par with those of the scholar, runs like a golden thread throughout the Chabad literature. Though the soul may differ in temperament, each Jewish man and woman, according to Chabad, possesses the ability to reach the highest perfection in the worship of G-d and in unity with Him.

Chabad has gone even further than that, teaching that in many respects the simple, unlearned worshiper, unaware of the esoteric or even elementary principles, has an advantage over the scholar. In fact, this advantage is twofold. In the first place, the unlearned Jew possesses natural humility, which is greater than the scholar's; and in the second place, it is possible for him to attain the very heights of passionate worship which are often beyond the reach of the cool, intellectual scholar.

The leaders of Chabad-Lubavitch have always praised the simplicity and sincerity of worship of the ordinary Jew, even though he or she may be quite unlearned. They have openly expressed their sincere admiration and envy of these qualities, possession of which is almost exclusively the privilege of the non-scholar.[12] There is, for example, the famous Chasidic story of the young illiterate Jewish farmer who attended Yom Kippur service in the synagogue of the Baal Shem Tov, but could not recite the prayers. His inner yearning for communion with G-d, however, was so deeply

---

12. *Some Aspects of Chabad Chassidism* (*On the Study of Chasidus*, p. 15).

aroused that he gave it expression in the only outlet of which he was capable, a passionate outburst of a "cock-a-doodle-do!" along with the shout "G-d have mercy!" which re-sounded throughout the synagogue. Yet, this unusual form of "worship," according to this story, saved the fate of the entire community![13] There are many similar stories which enjoy great prominence in Chasidic lore.

It was this principle of Chasidism, focusing on sincerity in Divine worship, and carrying with it the idea that the *am haaretz* can be as good and sometimes even a better worshiper than the scholar, that aroused some of the severest criticism and antagonism on the part of the Talmudic scholars of that age, who saw in it a threat to the authority of the Torah scholar. The fact that Chasidism, particularly Chabad, continually emphasized the importance of the study of the Torah, did not alleviate their fears.

At a public debate which took place in Minsk in the year 5543 (1783) between the scholars of Vilna, Shklov, Brisk and Minsk on the one hand, representing the opposition, and Rabbi Schneur Zalman, the founder of Chabad, on the other,[14] the latter was taken to task for the above-mentioned view. Rabbi Schneur Zalman effectively rejected their criticism, and in fact caused many of the opponents to become devout followers of Chasidism by his reply.

This principle, Rabbi Schneur Zalman explained, is based on the first Divine Revelation to Moses, the first leader of Israel, out of the burning bush (Exodus 3:2), which was Moses' first and most important lesson in true leadership of the Jewish people. According to the Baal Shem Tov's interpretation, the "burning bush that was not consumed" symbolizes the humble Jew, who is burning with a passionate

13. R. Yosef Y. Schneersohn of Lubavitch, *Igrot Kodesh*, vol. 5, p. 437.
14. See *Reshimat R. Yosef Y. Schneersohn of Lubavitch*, Issue 5, "*Vikuach Hagadol B'Minsk—5543,*" at length. In English—*Branches of the Chassidic Menorah*, vol. 1, p. 99 ff (SIE Publications, 1998).

fire of love for G-d, a fire which, like that of the bush's, is insatiable. Whereas the scholar's passionate worship of G-d finds an outlet through his prayers and study of the Torah—which he is able to understand and which enable him to blend his passionate feelings with the coolness of his intellectual understanding—the less educated Jew continues to be consumed by the fire of his passionate yearning to cleave to G-d—without being able to quench it. It is out of this humble "bush" that the "voice of G-d speaks"; it is among these humble but sincere folk that the Divine presence rests![15]

It follows, therefore, that no Jew need be disheartened from his desire to become a true worshiper of G-d by his lack of knowledge. It is not the theory but the deed that is most important. The primary requirements are sincerity and faith, and these are not lacking in any Jewish man or woman. For every Jew, by reason of his Divine soul, is imbued with an innate faith in G-d and His Torah, which, provided it is not kept under continuous suppression, easily asserts itself. If we begin to practice the Divine *mitzvot* with sincerity and faith, we will get a different outlook on life; our intellect will be considerably stimulated, and our intellectual capacity greatly enhanced. For just as physical food invigorates the physical body, so does spiritual food—the Torah and *mitzvot*—invigorate the soul. And just as physical food invigorates the body, whether or not we know how the digestive process takes place, so it is with the soul.

The Jewish way of life is: practice the Divine commandments with faith and sincerity, without waiting until you understand their significance. To say "I will not observe the commandments until I understand their significance" is the same as to say "I will not eat until I understand the process of digestion."[16]

This is the meaning of *naaseh v'nishma*—we will *do* (first)

15. *Sefer Hasichot 5702*, p. 47 ff.
16. *Sefer Hasichot 5680*, p. 5.

and (then) we will (try to) *understand*, the words which sig-
nified the Jewish people's acceptance of the Torah at Mount
Sinai.

SUMMARY: The notion that one need not be learned in
Torah to be a sincere and devout worshiper was developed
by Chabad in opposition to the traditional view of Jewish
scholars. Any Jew has the capacity to have complete faith in
G-d and the desire to do His will. All Jews have an inward
love of our Creator; even seemingly unobservant Jews have
sacrificed their lives to sanctify G-d's name.

Needless to say, Chabad strongly emphasizes and en-
courages Torah learning, which can only strengthen our connection to G-d.

INDEX

in merit of the Jewish Campus
that with Hashem's help
will be built very soon.

נדבת

התי יונתן מיכאל הלוי

וזוגתו נתני׳ פריידא רחל

אייברמס

לזכות יוצאי חלציהם

חנה

מוסיא

מאשא פרומא

מנחם מענדל הלוי

לוי יצחק הלוי

שלום דובער הלוי

דבורה לאה

שיחיו לאורך ימים ושנים טובות

ולהצלחה רבה ומופלגה

בגשמיות וברוחניות

בכל אשר יפנו

ולעילוי נשמת

מרת **חנה חי׳ שרה** בת **אברהם** ע״ה

טעמעקולא, קאליפורניא